Oysters

Oysters

A TRUE DELICACY

SHIRLY LINE

MACMILLAN·USA

Notes

Standard level spoon measurements are used in all recipes.

Eggs should be medium unless otherwise stated.

Milk should be whole milk unless otherwise stated.

All butter is sweet unless otherwise stated.

Ovens should be preheated to the specified temperature – if using a fan-assisted oven, follow the manufacturer's instructions for adjusting the time and the temperature.

Discard any oysters that are open before you come to eat or cook them, and any that do not open once cooked.

Art Director: **Jacqui Small**

Executive Art Editor: **Penny Stock**

Executive Editor: **Susan Haynes**

Editor: **Sasha Judelson**

Photography: **James Merrell**

Stylist: **Sue Skeen**

Home Economist: **Bridget Sargeson**

MACMILLAN
A Simon & Schuster Macmillan Company
1633 Broadway
New York, NY 10019-6785
First published in 1995 by Reed Consumer Books Limited

Library of Congress Cataloging-in-Publication Data available.

ISBN 0-02-860376-1

Produced by Mandarin Offset
Printed and bound in China

10 9 8 7 6 5 4 3 2 1

With great pleasure I dedicate this book to oyster lovers everywhere, and also to the oceans and seas around the world, the truly mighty forces that dictate the availability, size, nutritional value and beauty of this also mighty little mollusk.

CONTENTS

Introduction **7**

Appearances **9**

American Oysters **10**

Oyster Curiosities **16**

Serving Oysters **20**

What to Drink with Oysters **23**

The Recipes **25**

Index **64**

INTRODUCTION

There are two recognized oyster species: the *ostrea* and the *crassostrea*. To simplifiy, *ostrea* are mostly native oysters; whereas *crassostrea* have most commonly been introduced to the area.

Both oyster species include many varieties. The smallest change in location or turn of the tide can affect the flavor, size and shape of any oyster and often when that happens, it is given a new name, so adding to the ever-growing list of oysters.

The *ostrea (edulis)* can be known as a European flat, Belon, Dorset or Whitstable. The Olympia oyster has the slightly different tag of *ostrea (lurida)*. On the East Coast the *crassostrea (virginica)* is the dominant and native oyster species, with the names Bluepoint, Louisiana and Chincoteagues being particularly well known. On the West Coast the *crassostrea (gigas)*, sometimes with the prefix *Pacific*, takes over. It was originally imported from Japan in the early 1900s, as Portugese *crassostrea (angulata)*, to replenish emptied stocks of the Olympia.

APPEARANCES

Always buy oysters from a reputable supplier and check that the shells are tightly shut. A live and really fresh oyster uses the top and bottom muscles to hold the shell securely closed, especially when it hears somebody approaching with an oyster knife. When not feeling too well, the oyster will be too weak to hold the muscles tight and the shell will gape open: Don't eat it – throw it away!

To open oysters easily, heat them in a preheated oven 400°F for about 5 minutes, then plunge them into iced water and drain. Alternatively, microwave them on High for about 20 seconds, depending on their size or prise the shells apart with an oyster knife.

Shelled oysters should be plump and sweet-smelling. The liquor (love potion) should be clear, and always used or drunk. To store oysters, please do not toss them into a bucket of water: They hate it and will die! Store with the deep cup down, in a refrigerator or cool, airy place: oysters need oxygen if they are alive. Cover with a damp cloth or seaweed to prevent them from drying out and opening. The temperature should be no higher than 34°F. Oysters should be eaten no later than the day after purchase. The old adage that you should only eat oysters when there is an "r" in the month relates to *ostrea edulis* and arose because this species spawns in the summer months (May to August). Although there is nothing to stop you eating *edulis* oysters at this time, they tend to be gritty and not very plump and so are generally left to replenish stocks. *Crassostrea* oysters do not spawn in their shells and therefore are available all year round; but they can be a little "milky" when the weather is very warm.

AMERICAN OYSTERS

There are certainly more exotically named oysters in America than in any other country in the world – perhaps over a hundred from north to south. One traditional American oyster delicacy, dating back to before 1934, is *Roast "Saddle Rocks" in their Shells*. The author of the recipe is unknown, but the method is as follows: take as many oysters as required, making sure that all are tightly closed, and scrub the shells in sea water. Then place, deep-shelled side down, one at a time on a bed of hot coals or, better still, charcoal. As soon as the shells open, remove the top one of each, taking care not to spill any liquor. Place on heated plates for guests to season.

CHESAPEAKE BAY OYSTERS
(Crassostrea virginica)

The states of Virginia and Maryland together make up what has always been reputed to be the largest oyster producing area in the world. This section of the Atlantic coast has always produced a richly flavored, fat oyster. The first English settlers were saved from starvation in 1610 with a diet of Chesapeake Bay oysters, even though a dozen oysters have only 120 calories when consumed raw. The Chesapeake Bay oyster is small and makes an ideal cocktail snack when fried in batter. It is very good for cooking because the mild flavor needs a gentle boost to add a little zip. Hence the old favorite Chesapeake Stew, where the flavor of the oysters is enhanced with fresh celery. Try cooking the Chesapeake Bay oyster in a creamy sauce until the edges of the oyster curl, then pour the sauce onto fresh pasta – kids just love their oysters cooked this way. Chesapeake Bay oysters should be available year round.

MAD RIVER OYSTERS
(Crassostrea gigas)

From the warm waters of California comes a Pacific oyster that is robust in flavor, slightly salty and a good all rounder for enjoying uncooked on the half shell, smoked on the barbecue, in a *Carpetbag Steak* (see page 50), or in any recipe that would be enhanced by a subtle taste of the sea.

Mad River Oysters are familiar to all oyster growers on the California coastline. Not only do they have a strong fruity aftertaste which lingers, but it is reputed that they contain high levels of a number of vitamins and minerals, no doubt due to the rich plankton on which the oysters feed in the wonderful clear warm waters.

Unlike the Preston Point oyster (which is also grown in Californian waters), which sports a spiky tiger-striped shell, the shell of the Mad River oyster is somewhat smoother and rather more refined, while the shell of another Californian cousin, the Tomales Bay oyster, is almost black in color. You should be able to buy most varieties of Californian oysters at any time of the year.

APALACHICOLA OYSTERS
(Crassostrea virginica)

Apalachicola Bay in the northwest corner of Florida provides an excellent feeding ground for this plump sweet-flavored oyster with a greenish, deep-curved shell. The flesh is firm and slightly salty, and there is a tang of copper to create an added interest.

Use the Florida Gulf oysters, meat and juice, in a stew. They are smaller than the Apalachicola and quite creamy; ideal for sauces, dressings, pies and baked dishes. The deep shell of the Apalachicola is perfect for all recipes that require the oyster to be served free-standing in its shell, and oyster aficionados from around the world have enjoyed creating toppings which range from the simple to the exotic.

It is possible, since Apalachicola Bay is so close to New Orleans, that these deep-shelled oysters were the inspiration for that most famous of oyster recipes – *Oysters à la Rockfeller*. Jules Alciatore, chef of the famous restaurant Antoine's, created this oyster classic with a wealth of rich ingredients in 1900 and named it after the multimillionaire. Antoine's still fiercely guard the original recipe but it has been interpreted and adapted many times and in many cookbooks, including this one (see page 60).

TOMALES BAY OYSTERS
(Crassostrea gigas)

The rich, clear waters of California produce an abundant supply of oysters, which complement their beautiful environmentally friendly waters with a clear, cool, slightly salty taste.

The Californian Tomales Bay oyster is readily recognizable by its deep-cupped, almost black, frilly shell. This oyster should be tried by the first-timer at a cocktail bar because it is so gentle and loving toward the palate, and because from a health point of view it is so much better to get addicted to than salted peanuts.

WESTCOTT BAY OYSTERS
(Ostrea edulis and Crassostrea gigas)

It is possible these oysters were once delivered, at peak growing time, to the White House: Rumor had it that oysters were the preferred brain food of President Roosevelt when he had major problems.

From Tiger Bay to Westcott Bay, both European flats (*ostrea edulis*) and *crassostrea gigas* oysters are grown – they all qualify as Westcott Bay oysters.

Only a limited number of *ostrea edulis* are grown, but the few that do get to the tables of people who are prepared to pay for them are superb. They have a flavor that is delicate and difficult to adequately describe.

Westcott Bay *edulis* oysters have a round, flat shell with a shallow cup to hold very concentrated liquor. They must be served with loving care and perhaps a little squeeze of lemon. The Westcott Bay *crassostrea gigas* oyster has a very deep cup, and although quite round in shape, it is deeply ridged, revealing how many years it has taken to grow. Three to four years would be the optimum age for a *gigas* oyster – the *edulis* takes a little longer to reach maturity.

The *gigas* from this area are always sweet and full in flavor, with not too much of a salty taste. The smaller oysters, around 2 ounces, are ideal to serve with cocktails; oysters that weigh over 4 ounces are enhanced with a well-flavored butter sauce seasoned with salt and paprika.

PORTUGUESE OYSTERS
(Crassostrea angulata)

The story goes – and it could easily be true – that in the early eighteenth century, oysters were brought to Portugal from Japan, clinging to the bottom of the wooden boats of the explorers. They became known as *ostrea angulata* and rapidly established themselves in Portugal. In 1866, with many oysters that had stowed away from Japan still hanging-in on its hull, one of the Portuguese wooden ships went aground in a storm off the coast of France. The stowaways survived to multiply by the million. (This must prove that these oysters are tough fellas to not only survive the storm, but also to be wise enough to set up new homes in strange waters).

How the *ostrea angulata* arrived in America I have no idea – it must have been on another wooden boat – but arrive they did, and soon became established from Vancouver to Colombia on the West Coast.

Sizes can vary, but Portuguese oysters are always rather on the large size, housing a meat that is nutty in flavor and plump. If left to grow for more than five years the shell could be six inches across. The deep cup is ideal for recipes that require the oyster to be served in the shell. I prefer this oyster cooked. The meat is not delicate and it is definitely a mashed potato and beer job, rather than champagne.

BRETON SOUND OYSTERS
(Crassostrea virginica)

The Breton Sound oyster is a Louisiana oyster growing in the wild and is in plentiful supply in the Wild Reef area.

The taste of the Breton Sound oyster will vary in saltiness. This is due to fresh river waters sweeping the estuaries in the spring, when the Mississippi flood waters attack the oyster beds; at this time of year the Breton Sound oysters are plump with a delectable sweetish flavor. For the remaining part of the year they take a more salty flavor from the sea water surrounding the beds.

The fatty texture of Louisiana oysters must mean they are full of Omega 3 fish oils, that benefit the heart.

BELON OYSTERS
also known as European Flat
(Ostrea edulis)

The Belon is the president of all oysters, so the price is always high. Unlike the *Crassostrea gigas* species, the Belon spawns in warm waters during the summer months. For reasons of conservation, this species of oyster must be left to replenish its stocks during summer, thus validating the quotation: "Never eat oysters when there is no 'r' in the month."

The Belon is round, with a flat, shallow shell. It has a flavor that is both sweet and slightly salty; quite magical. For the true gourmet, to introduce any other texture or flavor to the Belon is sacrilege. It should not be cooked. The recognized season for Belons is from September to May.

Pictured right

TOTTEN OYSTERS
(Pacific gigas)

The Totten oyster comes from one of the United States' most productive growing areas, Puget Sound, in Washington, where it grows alongside the Belon, Olympia, Oyster Bay, and Shelton oysters.

Oysters grow fast in the algae-rich inlets of Puget Sound, which is well known as a great seafood area. When mature, the Totten is a sophisticated full-flavored little oyster which is very plump and wonderful for cooking.

Pictured left

KUMAMOTO OYSTERS
(from the *Crassostrea gigas* species)
In 1568 Job Hortop set down in the Gulf of Mexico and wrote of "oysters growing on trees." ' The story goes that spat (baby oysters) clung in bunches to trees on the water's edge. The oysters were alternately covered in water or left high and dry, with the tide, thus encouraging them to grow well. Today a more conventional method of oyster farming produces a smooth tasting oyster. The flavor is sweet, and not salty. The Kumamoto is found from the Gulf of Mexico to British Columbia and should be available all year. The meat of the Kumamoto oyster has a greenish tint, with a delicate and soft buttery texture. Although excellent for any oyster recipe, this prized oyster is perfection when served simply. The Kumamoto needs two drops of lemon juice only, nothing harsh, which would kill the delicate flavor. Enjoy it with a semi-sweet wine.
Pictured right

OLYMPIA OYSTERS
(*Ostrea lurida*)
A small, exciting little oyster that originally grew wild in the waters of California and upwards to the frozen north, just proving how tough he or she was. Originally the Olympia oyster was the most popular oyster in California. The Olympia oyster is now tamed and farmed. It is a round and tiny little oyster with a flat shell. It still has a good strong flavor, with a distinct aftertaste to linger, just as a good wine would. This oyster is far too interesting to cook. Enjoy it with a squeeze of lemon and a cool Chardonnay, as you would the "Fines de claires" of France.
Pictured left

LOUISIANA OYSTERS
(Crassostrea virginica)

Ranking top in national oyster production, the extensive Louisiana beds – from the public grounds to the privately owned stretches of warm Gulf waters – provide a continuous top quality supply of oysters twelve months of the year. The taste will vary in saltiness during the year, due to fresh river waters sweeping the estuaries in the Spring when the Mississippi flood waters attack the oyster beds; at this time of year the oysters are plump with a delectable sweetish flavor. For the rest of the year they take on a more salty flavor from the sea water surrounding the beds. The fatty texture of Louisiana oyster must mean they are high in Omega 3 fatty acids, that benefit the heart.

Pictured left

WELLFLEET OYSTERS
(Crassostrea virginica)

In 1606 Samuel de Champlain found the most perfect growing area for oysters: Wellfleet, Massachusetts. These magical waters were and still are fed by several small rivers and fresh water springs, surrounded by salt marshes which contribute just the right amount of flavor.

This is still a perfect growing area and for all the same reasons and because it has an average daily tidal range of 10 foot.

Not really for cooking, they should be eaten with just a squeeze of lemon and a dry white cocktail, or a medium sweet champagne. The flavor can be fairly salty with a fine sweet aftertaste.

Pictured right

TEXAS GULF OYSTERS
(Crassostrea virginica)

This is a big oyster with a robust and distinctive meaty flavor; a great oyster to top a big fat juicy steak. There is nothing really exciting to say about the appearance of the Texas Gulf oyster; it can be round to oblong in shape, depending on how many times it has been moved by the tides when growing and is no way as sexy to look at as its pretty friend from Tomales Bay, with its black frilly shell.

The meat of the Texas Gulf oyster can be quite salty. It is a firm oyster, quite a mouthful to chew, which makes it ideal for cooking. Try tossing it on the barbecue for a summer party – it will taste great because the rich meat will plump up further when introduced to direct heat; and you have something firm to stick your skewer into every time.

Pictured left

BON SECOUR OYSTERS
(Crassostrea virginica)

At the start of the twentieth century Chris Nelson's grandfather gathered thousands of meaty little oysters which at that time were growing wild in the Bon Secour waters of Alabama. The turn of the tide, a simple natural phenomenon, depleted those stocks.

Chris Nelson has now turned that tide once again; digging deep into the Bon Secour Bay, he has found off-bottom cultured oysters.

Bon Secour Bay oysters are sweet and not too salty. Ideal for such things as Texas Fries.

Good luck to you, Chris Nelson, your grandpa would be proud.

Pictured right

OYSTER CURIOSITIES

The Aphrodite Inheritance

Oysters have always been linked with love. When Aphrodite, the Greek goddess of love, sprang forth from the sea on an oyster shell and promptly gave birth to Eros, the word "aphrodisiac" was also born.

Richly laden tables of asparagus, snails and ostrich brain were dictated as the staple diet for the infamous Roman orgies from around 5 BC, with no great feast being complete without the prized delights for lust and pleasure: Oysters.

Around 76 AD, the Roman Emperor Vitellus, famed for eating oysters continuously throughout the day and night, ordered thousands of slaves to gather *ostrea edulis* oysters from the south coast of England. He had the oysters transported to Rome to feed members of the imperial court and guests alike; never before had such a humble living creature aroused such passionate feelings. Vitellus preferred oysters to grapes, while the ladies of the court enjoyed their oysters most of all when dipped in honey.

The history of the oyster is rich with subtle and pleasurable nuances. Although Aristotle thought the oyster to have "no sensation of sex," Apuleius, famed for his work *The Golden Ass*, written in 125 AD, reputedly made a love potion of oysters with which to seduce Aemilia, and look what oysters did for Casanova: It is said that he consumed up to about 60 oysters a day. American men should follow the legendary Italian lover and eat more oysters. National health guidelines suggest that 15 mg of zinc should be included in the male diet, and oysters are the ideal food to provide the zinc needed to improve male fertility.

Pharmacologically, the true aphrodisiac capacity of an oyster really depends on the dopamine content. This is a vital neurotransmitter that helps to govern brain activity and influence sexual desire. Dopamine provokes sexual interest and triggers responses, while improving performance in both males and females. It is said to amplify the intensity of sensation.

Health and Nutrition

Often posed questions include: Are oysters good for you? Do oysters improve your health? One thing is for sure, with approximately 75 calories in 12 oysters and a guarantee that they will improve your sex life, a dozen to replace a meal twice a day for a week could have the most fantastic results!

All fish and shellfish contain natural polyunsaturated oils – known as Omega 3 fatty acids – recognized by medical experts as fundamental for good health. These essential fish oils play a role in maintaining clear arteries, and are also of benefit to the central nervous system. It is true that the bigger and fatter the oysters, the bigger the helping of Omega 3, but these oils are now regarded as of more benefit than risk for those suffering with a little too much cholesterol.

When asked why he ate oysters in a restaurant when he adhered to Jewish dietary laws and shunned shellfish in his home, a charming 98-year-old Jewish gentleman declared: "I only indulge in my three dozen oysters a week at the Oyster Bar because my doctor recommends them for a long life and happy heart." Indeed, a 2-ounce oyster could soon be rocking the salted peanut from its stool at the café, cocktail bar, bistro or tapas bar.

Nutritional Values

Oysters contain the following vitamins: A, B1, B2, C and D. Minerals include: calcium, iodine, magnesium, iron, potassium, copper, sodium, zinc, phosphorus, manganese and sulfur. Forget the vitamin and mineral pills, just eat a dozen oysters! On very rare occasions, oysters may contain harmful microbes. The Food and Drug Administration estimates that 5 percent of shellfish, including oysters, contain *vibrio vulnificus* bacteria, which could cause people suffering from allergies, diabetes, AIDS or other diseases to become quite ill. Cooking kills the bacteria, as does serving the oysters with a spicy hot sauce (according to a research team at Louisiana State University). Dr. Charles Saunders told the *New York Times*: "I still eat plenty of oysters, but I do like my hot sauce."

The biggest concern with all shellfish remains just how long they have been hanging around. Wherever, whatever, buy your oysters from a reputable supplier, and when eating out, choose a restaurant known for the freshness of its fish and the rapidity of its turnover.

History

Oysters have been an important food since Neolithic times. They were cultivated in China before the Christian era, the Greeks served them with wine and the Romans were so enthusiastic about these marvelous mollusks that they sent thousands of slaves to the shores of the English Channel to gather oysters. English oysters were so highly prized by Roman generals that they paid for them by their weight in gold. The biggest expense, however, as it is today, was the cost of transportation across the sea and then over the Alps. The oysters were packed in snow-covered barrels to keep them alive during transportation.

The Native Americans were great lovers of the oyster too, as is evidenced by the millons of shells that archeologists have discovered. When the Native Americans got hooked on oysters four thousand years ago, they felt it too cannibalistic to eat the creatures alive, so they invented oyster stew.

Oysters were an important – and inexpensive – part of the diet in Britain from the Middle Ages through to the nineteenth century. It was estimated that 700 million oysters a year were eaten in London alone in 1864. Chaucer, Shakespeare, Byron and Charles Dickens extolled the virtues of the oyster. The famous *Diary* written by Samuel Pepys in the seventeenth century contains several references, including a description of a New Year's breakfast that featured a barrel of oysters. By the end of the nineteenth century, however, oysters had become rarer and much more costly, due to increasing demand and overdredging of the natural oyster beds, and plans were put in motion for the establishment of the first British artifical oyster beds.

In 1910 the United States led the world in terms of oyster yields with 26,800,000 bushels, with France lying in second place with 3,250,000 bushels. From Texas to Cape Cod, overharvesting and uncontrollable diseases depleted the stocks later. The good news today must be that after a lapse in oyster production, due to problems of pollution as well as overfishing and disease, things are picking up. The future could be something to really cheer about, and the famous oyster-opening competition in St Mary's County Oyster Festival, Maryland, could be bigger than ever.

Oysters commence life as male, and then decide after 12 months that they prefer to be female. Although a rich diet and warm waters dictate that oysters remain female, the female oyster likes to revert back to being male after spawning. The male oyster also goes through the process of childbirth, laying as many as 1 million eggs a year, just like the female oyster.

SERVING OYSTERS

In France oysters are served on a large platter of crushed ice. The oysters are left in the shell with the bottom muscle uncut, and still attached to the shell, to allow the customer to see that they are fresh. Elsewhere they may be served with the top muscle cut, the top shell discarded and the bottom muscle also cut to allow the oyster to be turned in the shell before serving – because many people feel that this is a prettier sight.

Do not cook tiny oysters; They will shrivel down to become tiny black spots and will lose much of their original taste.

For a dinner party allow six fresh oysters per person and serve on individual plates of crushed ice. Select oysters of a similar size. Open them just before serving, removing the top shell. Serve with oyster forks and wedges of lemon.

There are two terms often referred to when discussing oysters. The first is shucking, which is opening the shell and removing the oyster; the other is scrubbing, which is scrubbing the empty oyster shell.

It is not true that you eat the oyster alive, because immediately after the shell is pried apart and oxygen enters, the oyster will die; and with a squeeze of lemon it will have the last wriggle.

WHAT TO DRINK WITH OYSTERS

Champagne is a must if the oysters are of the native species (*ostrea edulis* or European flats). Oz Clarke, a noted authority on wine, once wrote that he felt the champagne was more of an aphrodisiac than the oyster. Mimosa (a mixture of orange juice and champagne) would be wonderful if serving oysters for breakfast or brunch.

If you indulge in oysters in Ireland or at a party where the host is Irish, no doubt you will be treated to wonderful Black Velvet (champagne and Guinness).

It is not really necessary to serve an expensive white wine with oysters. If the wine is exceptional, it will steal the whole show from the oysters. A bottle of Muscadet is a choice with which you cannot go far wrong. I used to enjoy Californian, French, or Australian Chardonnay, in particular the rich woody flavor of the Napa family or Australian range, but again I think I would prefer something to drink that is not as distinctive in taste; do not forget the seaweedy, salty, mineral taste with which the wine will have to compete.

A tall glass of Spanish dry sherry taken straight from the refrigerator is perfect with all shellfish, especially oysters.

A word of warning: Never drink whiskey, brandy or other strong spirits with or after eating oysters. They react together in the stomach and both will be rejected in quite an unpleasant way.

THE RECIPES

Oysters *au naturel* are best served simply, with crushed ice and seaweed or salsify (also called oyster plant). Fresh lemon juice or Worcestershire sauce are both good accompaniments. A connoisseur will tell you that Tabasco is too strong and will kill the delicate flavor of a good oyster. There are two classic sauces to be served with oysters. The first is mignonnette sauce, a combination of 1 chopped shallot, juice of ½ a lemon, 6 tablespoons of red wine vinegar and freshly ground black pepper. The second, chili sauce, is a variation on mignonette sauce. Make as above with the addition of 2 seeded and finely chopped green chilies, 4 sprigs of fresh cilantro, finely chopped, and a pinch of sugar. Both sauces should be kept refrigerated. Fresh oysters may be frozen for up to 3 months. Do not remove them from the freezer within 24 hours of freezing. Allow 55 minutes to thaw and then serve immediately.

ANGELS ON HORSEBACK

This simple and tasty recipe for oysters became popular in the nineteenth century and has remained so ever since. When oysters were not available, scallops were used instead and the recipe appeared on the menu as *Archangels on Horseback*. I have never been able to understand how or why "horses" became associated with this dish and am still waiting to find out!

Open as many Pacific oysters as you will need, reserving the liquor. Wrap each oyster in a slice of bacon and secure with a wooden toothpick. Cook under a fairly hot broiler or on the barbecue, turning until the bacon is crispy. Remove from the broiler or barbecue and then roll in a generous amount of fine fried breadcrumbs or place on crisp warm toast, before serving with a garnish of watercress.

Or try *The Poacher's Breakfast*, a recipe created by the oyster dredgers of the English Kent coast over fifty years ago. The working men would always sneak a few oysters into their pockets while out at sea. Breakfast on board the oyster smack (boat) would consist of the forbidden fruit concealed in bacon and then fried in bacon fat with a couple of eggs cracked in the pan for good measure.

"But four young Oysters hurried up,
All eager for the treat:
Their coats were brushed, their faces washed,
Their shoes were clean and neat—
And this was odd, because, you know,
They hadn't any feet."

Lewis Carroll *Alice Through the Looking Glass*

OYSTER AND CAVIAR CANAPÉS

as much caviar as you can afford

8 oysters – Olympia oysters (*ostrea edulis*)

juice of 1 lemon

freshly ground black pepper

finely chopped parsley, to garnish

2 lemons, quartered, to serve

Tartlet Shells

1½ cups all-purpose flour

2 tablespoons shortening

¼ cup/½ stick butter

pinch of salt

6–7 tablespoons iced water

Make the tartlet shells. Put the flour in a mixing bowl, cut in the fats and rub them in until the mixture resembles fine breadcrumbs. Add the salt, then mix in the water a little at a time until the mixture forms a firm dough. Wrap the pastry in plastic wrap and allow it to rest in the refrigerator for 30 minutes.

Preheat the oven to 375°F. Roll out the pastry thinly on a lightly floured surface to line 8 greased round or boat-shaped molds, measuring about 2½ inches. Prick the pastry all over with a fork, line with nonstick baking paper and fill with dried or pastry beans. Bake for 10 minutes. Remove the paper and beans, then carefully remove the pastry shells and leave to cool on a wire rack.

Just before serving, divide the caviar equally between the cooled pastry shells. Open the oysters, reserving the liquor for use in another recipe. Top each caviar-filled pastry shell with an oyster and sprinkle lightly with lemon juice. Garnish with parsley and serve with lemon wedges. Offer a pepper mill at the table.

Serves 4

OYSTER CHOWDER

10 ounces lean pork, cut into bite-sized pieces

1 onion, chopped

3 stalks celery, diced

1 green bell pepper, seeded and diced

4 potatoes, diced

1¼ cups fish stock

2½ cups milk

24 big oysters (anything but native *ostrea edulis* or Belons)

juice of 1 lemon

3 tablespoons all-purpose flour

¼–⅓ cup/½–¾ stick butter, softened

1 cup dry white vermouth

12 small clams (in their shells, shells scrubbed)

salt and pepper

paprika, to garnish

Heat the pork gently in a saucepan until the fat runs, raise the heat, add the onion and sauté for 3 minutes. Add the celery, green bell pepper, potatoes and fish stock, cook for 3 minutes, then stir in the milk, season to taste. Bring to the boil and simmer until the pork cubes and vegetables are cooked through. Open the oysters, adding the liquor to the pan with the lemon juice. In a small bowl, mix the flour and butter to a paste; add a small amount at a time to the simmering liquid, stirring thoroughly each time, until the sauce thickens. Stir in the vermouth. Add the clams and fold in the oysters. Simmer for 2 minutes so the clams open. (Discard any that remain shut.) Serve with a sprinkling of paprika.

Serves 4–6

OYSTER AND GUINNESS SOUP

Do not use too big an oyster for this soup; medium-sized Pacific *gigas* are ideal.

½ cup/1 stick butter

1 onion, chopped

⅔ cup dry white wine

½ cup all-purpose flour

1¼ cups fish stock or court bouillon

24 oysters

1¼ cups Guinness (or other dark beer)

⅔ cup heavy cream

salt and pepper

plenty of finely chopped parsley, to garnish

Melt half of the butter in a saucepan, add the onion and fry until softened. Pour in the wine, bring to simmering point and simmer for 3 minutes.

Meanwhile melt the remaining butter in a separate saucepan, stir in the flour and cook for 1 minute. Gradually add the fish stock or court bouillon, stirring constantly until you have a creamy sauce to add to the wine and onions. Mix well, then add salt and pepper to taste.

Open the oysters, adding the liquor to the soup. Pour the Guinness into the soup and stir constantly until it reaches boiling point. Reduce the heat to low, stir in the cream and then fold in the oysters with loving care. Continue to cook over a low heat for 1 minute only before serving in heated soup bowls.

Garnish with chopped parsley.

Serves 4–6

OYSTER CHIPS

These make an excellent lunchtime snack.

36 medium oysters

oil, for deep frying

Batter

½ cup all-purpose flour

2 eggs, beaten

1¼ cups milk

grated nutmeg

salt and pepper

Place the oysters in a large heavy-bottomed saucepan over a moderate heat. Cover tightly and steam the oysters, shaking the saucepan frequently, until they open. Discard any that remain shut. Drink the oyster liquor or reserve it for use in another recipe. Remove the oysters from the shells and pat them dry with paper towels. Set aside.

Make the batter. Mix the flour and eggs in a bowl. Gradually beat in the milk until the mixture forms a smooth coating batter. Add nutmeg, salt and pepper to taste.

Gently drop the oysters into the batter, carefully rolling them around until they are evenly coated.

In a large, deep saucepan, heat the oil for deep frying to 350–375°F or until a cube of bread added to the oil browns in 30 seconds. Fry the battered oysters, one at a time. Each oyster takes only a few seconds – it will take only 1 minute to cook all 36 oysters, give or take a few seconds. Using a slotted spoon, transfer the cooked oysters to paper towels to drain, then pile into a warm serving dish and serve at once.

Serves 4-6

MARINATED OYSTERS AND SALMON

This is highly suitable as an hors d'œuvre. Use a medium-sized oyster with a firm meat content, which is not too salty. *Crassostrea gigas* or *virginica* oysters are ideal. Because the salmon is not cooked, it is important that it be fresh and from a reputable source.

24 oysters

1 pound fresh salmon, boned

Marinade

1¼ cups dry white wine

6 tablespoons fresh orange juice

2 tablespoons soy sauce

1 tablespoon sugar

12 drained capers

salt and pepper

Garnish

1 kiwi fruit, sliced (optional)

3–4 radicchio leaves, shredded

Prepare the marinade at least 1½ hours before you want to serve this dish. Combine all the marinade ingredients in a saucepan and bring to the boil. Remove from the heat and set aside to cool slightly. Open the oysters, adding the liquor to the marinade. Remove the oysters from their shell and place them on a flattish dish.

Trim the salmon and cut it into pieces the same size as the oysters. Arrange the pieces on the dish with the oysters and spoon the warm marinade over both. Leave until cold, then cover and chill in the refrigerator for 1 hour. Garnish with kiwi fruit, if using, and shredded radicchio leaves and serve.

Serves 6

OYSTER AND PUMPKIN SOUFFLÉS

This unusual combination makes an impressive appetizer. Use small, flavorsome oysters.

¼ cup/½ stick butter, plus extra for greasing

12 oysters

¼ cup all-purpose flour

1 cup finely mashed cooked pumpkin

pinch of cayenne pepper

4 eggs, separated

pinch of grated nutmeg, or to taste

salt and pepper

watercress to garnish (optional)

At least 1 hour in advance grease four 4-inch ovenproof ramekins and place them on a baking sheet in the freezer (this allows the soufflés to come away from the sides with ease). Preheat the oven to 400°F.

Open the oysters, reserving the liquor.

Melt the butter in a saucepan over a gentle heat, stir in the flour and cook for 1 minute. Add the mashed pumpkin and reserved oyster liquor, stirring constantly until thoroughly mixed. Add the cayenne, with salt and pepper to taste. Remove the saucepan from the heat and stir in the egg yolks, one at a time. Return to a low heat and stir constantly until the mixture thickens a little more and is smooth.

Whisk the egg whites in a grease-free bowl until stiff; gently fold them into the pumpkin mixture using a metal spoon. As soon as the mixture is blended, spoon it into the prepared ramekins. Drop 3 oysters into each dish and dust with a little nutmeg.

Bake the soufflés for 20–25 minutes, until the tops are firm and golden. Serve immediately, garnished with watercress, if using; and don't wait for any late arrivals!

Serves 4

OYSTERS ROLAND JÖHRI – ST. MORITZ

This special dish is made in two stages. The recipe for the pasta shavings on which the oyster shells rest is on page 63. The pasta should be prepared first.

16 Olympia oysters (*ostrea edulis*)

¼ cup whipped cream or crème fraîche

I tablespoon dry white vermouth

2 tablespoons Chardonnay wine

I egg yolk, beaten

pinch of saffron

2 tablespoons butter

10 leaves of young fresh spinach, cut into strips

grated nutmeg, to taste

salt and pepper

Open the oysters, reserving the liquor in a saucepan. Set the oysters aside and scrub the bottom shells. Bring a saucepan of water to the boil, add the bottom shells and boil for 10 minutes. Drain and set aside. Add 2 tablespoons of the whipped cream or crème fraîche to the oyster liquor, together with the vermouth and the Chardonnay wine. Boil until reduced by half. Remove from the heat and stir in the beaten egg yolk, saffron and remaining cream or crème fraîche.

Melt the butter in a skillet, add the spinach and toss lightly until just tender. Season with nutmeg, salt and pepper. Toss the spinach with the pasta and spoon onto a large platter.

Arrange the oyster shells on the pasta mixture, return the oysters to their shells, and cover each oyster with the sauce. Pop under a hot broiler for just a few seconds, to warm the oysters.

Serves 4

BARLEY SALAD WITH OYSTERS

16 Belon oysters

fresh lemon juice

finely chopped chives, to garnish

chicory or corn salad, to serve

Barley Salad

¼ cup barley, soaked overnight in water to cover and drained

½ cup small zucchini, cut into small pieces

⅓ cup baby carrot, cut into small pieces

¾ cup scallions, cut into small pieces

I large tomato, skinned, seeded and cubed

Sherry Dressing

2 tablespoons sherry vinegar

2 tablespoons Dijon mustard

I tablespoon sherry

¼ cup cold pressed extra virgin olive oil

pinch of sugar

salt and pepper

Add the barley to a pan of boiling water and simmer for I hour or until tender. Drain and allow to cool. Mix the barley with all the salad vegetables. For the dressing, mix together the vinegar, mustard and sherry. Whisk in the oil, add sugar, salt and pepper to taste. Open the oysters, adding the liquor to the dressing. To serve, pour the dressing over the barley and vegetables; mix well. Divide the salad between 2 plates and top each with 8 oysters, adding lemon juice. Garnish with chives and chicory or corn salad.

Serves 2

CHILI GRILLED OYSTERS MEXICO WAY

Use an oyster that has a deep cup, such as the Portuguese oyster.

12 oysters

1 red chili, seeded and sliced, or chili paste to taste

½-inch piece of fresh ginger root, peeled and finely chopped

¼ cup fresh breadcrumbs

¼ cup/½ stick butter, softened

2–4 tablespoons white rum

sea salt (see method)

Open the oysters, reserving the liquor. Set the oysters aside and scrub the bottom shells. Bring a saucepan of water to the boil, add the bottom shells and boil for 10 minutes. Drain and set aside.

Using a pestle, pound the chili with the ginger in a mortar until smooth. Gradually mix in the breadcrumbs and reserved oyster liquor. Spoon the mixture into a bowl and stir in the butter until thoroughly mixed.

Add enough of the rum to make a spreadable mixture.

Cover a baking sheet with sea salt to hold the oyster shells without tipping. Return the oysters to the shells and cover each one with the chili-crumb mixture. Place the filled shells carefully on the salt-topped baking sheet and cook under a very hot broiler for about 2 minutes or until the breadcrumbs are nicely toasted. Serve at once.

Serves 4

OYSTER AND BEEF PÂTÉ

2 tablespoons butter

12 Pacific *gigas* oysters

¼ cup finely ground lean beef

⅓ cup finely chopped green bell pepper

1 shallot, finely chopped

1 teaspoon tomato paste

2 eggs, beaten

1 cup fresh breadcrumbs

salt and pepper

Garnish

¼ cup/½ stick butter

3 cups fresh mushrooms or 1 cup drained canned mushrooms, sliced

1 clove garlic, chopped

watercress

Preheat the oven to 350°F. Using the butter, generously grease 4 ovenproof ramekins. Open the oysters, reserving the liquor in a bowl. Remove the oysters, chop coarsely and add to the liquor together with the beef, green bell pepper and shallot. Mix well, and stir in the tomato paste, beaten eggs and breadcrumbs. Mix thoroughly, add salt and pepper to taste. Divide the mixture between the ramekins. Place in a roasting pan, pour in boiling water to 1 inch from the ramekin tops. Bake for 20 minutes.

Just before serving, prepare the garnish. Melt the butter in a skillet over a gentle heat, add the mushrooms and garlic and toss lightly until tender. Remove the ramekins from the *bain-marie*. Turn out onto 2 plates. Spoon half the mushroom mixture around each pair of pâtés and garnish with watercress. Serve at once.

Serves 2

BAKED OYSTERS AUSTRALIAN STYLE

The baked oysters can be prepared before guests arrive and served just warm.

2 tablespoons butter

2 cloves garlic, crushed

3 cups fresh wholemeal breadcrumbs

¼ cup crumbled blue cheese

48 large Pacific *gigas* or *virginica* oysters

⅔ cup sour cream

I teaspoon soy sauce

freshly ground black pepper

Garnish

2–3 tomatoes, sliced

shredded basil leaves

Preheat the oven to 400°F. Melt the butter in a saucepan, add the garlic, stir in the breadcrumbs and cook until crisp. Remove from the heat and add the cheese, with black pepper to taste.

Open the oysters, tipping the liquor into a bowl. Add the sour cream and soy sauce to the bowl and mix well. Remove the oysters from their shells and divide them between 8 individual gratin dishes. Spoon the sour cream mixture over the top and cover that with the cheese and breadcrumb mixture.

Bake for a maximum of 10 minutes, just long enough to brown the breadcrumbs. Serve with a garnish of sliced tomatoes sprinkled with shredded basil.

Serves 8

FORESTIÈRE OYSTERS

Use Apalachicola, Kumamoto or Chesapeake oysters for this recipe.

16 oysters (*gigas* or *virginica*)

3 cups fresh button mushrooms (or chanterelles for a special occasion)

2 tablespoons butter

scant ½ cup finely chopped shallots

juice of ½ lemon

1 tablespoon finely chopped parsley

2 tablespoons crème fraîche

½ cup Gruyère cheese, finely grated

freshly ground black pepper

Open the oysters, reserving the liquor. Remove the oysters from their shells and arrange in a shallow flameproof serving dish. Clean the button mushrooms by wiping them with paper towels; chop them very finely. If using chanterelles, rinse them briefly under cold water, drain and pat dry. Chop into small pieces. Melt the butter in a skillet, add the shallots and sauté for 1 minute. Stir in the mushrooms and lemon juice and cook for 1 minute more, then add the reserved oyster liquor with black pepper to taste. Stir in the parsley and crème fraîche.

Spoon some sauce over each oyster. Sprinkle with a little grated Gruyère. Place the dish under a preheated hot broiler until the cheese bubbles. Serve at once.

Serves 2

OYSTER PIES IN VINE LEAVES

Eight little pies to serve for a supper party or as an appetizer for 4. Use Pacific *gigas* oysters. Drained, blanched spinach leaves may be substituted for the vine leaves if preferred.

8 oysters, each about 3½–4½ ounces

8 vine leaves (see note above)

6 ounces puff pastry, thawed if frozen

½ cup/1 stick butter, softened

1¼ cups fresh white breadcrumbs

grated rind and juice of ½ lemon

2 tablespoons dry sherry

1 garlic clove, crushed

pinch of mace

beaten egg yolk, to glaze

Preheat the oven to 400°F. Open the oysters, reserving the liquor. Remove the oysters from their shell. Wash and steam or blanch fresh vine leaves until tender; if using vine leaves in brine, rinse them and gently pat them dry to remove any excess water. Wrap each oyster in a vine leaf to make a small neat parcel. Set aside.

On a lightly floured surface, roll out the puff pastry and use it to line 8 muffin pans, reserving sufficient pastry for 8 lids.

In a bowl, mix the softened butter with the breadcrumbs, lemon rind and juice, sherry, garlic and mace. Add the reserved oyster liquor. Divide the mixture between the pastry-lined muffin pans, top each with a wrapped oyster and seal with a pastry lid. Brush each pie with a little of the beaten egg yolk, make two small slits in the lid to allow the steam to escape and bake for 10 minutes only. Serve immediately.

Serves 4

CARPETBAG STEAK FOR THE BARBECUE

4 rump steaks, about 6 ounces each

16 small, sweet oysters

¼ cup/½ stick butter, softened

2 garlic cloves, crushed

2 tablespoons finely chopped parsley

freshly ground black pepper

Using a good sharp knife, slit each steak lengthwise to form a "pocket." Open the oysters, reserving the liquor for use in another recipe. In a bowl, mix the oysters with the butter, garlic and parsley.

Add pepper to taste.

Divide the oyster mixture evenly between the pockets in the steak. Close the openings with half a wooden kebab stick or metal skewer. Cook each steak on a lightly oiled barbecue; grill for the length of time that suits individual tastes.

Serves 4

Oysters are the richest animal source of vitamins and minerals.

JIFFY OYSTER FEAST

4½-quart container of oyster meat in its own liquor

½ bottle dry white wine

3 pounds cooked peeled shrimp, thawed if frozen

¾ cup dry sherry

a few black olives, to garnish

Saffron Rice

10 saffron threads

1 cup boiling water

¼ cup olive oil

generous 1 cup finely chopped onion

2 cloves garlic, crushed

2½ cups arborio (round grained) rice

1 quart fish stock

freshly ground black pepper

For the rice, pound the saffron to a powder. Stir in the water and set aside. Heat the oil in a saucepan, add the onion and garlic and sauté until translucent. Add the rice and stir until coated. Pour in the stock and saffron liquid. Bring to the boil, stir and cover. Cook for 30 minutes or until the rice is cooked. Meanwhile drain the oysters, tipping the liquor into a saucepan. Add the wine and bring to the boil, then simmer and add the shrimp. Cook for 2 minutes. Add the oysters and cook for 1 minute more. Remove the seafood. Bring the seafood liquid back to the boil and reduce by half. Remove from the heat and stir in the sherry and season with pepper. Fork the seafood into the warm rice and pour the sherry-flavored liquid on top. Garnish with olives.

Serves 12 (or fewer)

Burlington Arcade in London was built by Lord Cavendish, former owner of Burlington House. The Arcade was built to stop passersby from throwing their oyster shells into his garden.

OYSTERS ON TOAST

Use Pacific *gigas* or *virginica* oysters for this recipe, not the native *ostrea edulis* or the Belon, which it would be sacrilege to cook.

oysters, as many as you like

2–3 tablespoons butter, per 12 oysters

2 slices of bread, or more or less as desired

lemon wedges (optional)

Open the oysters, reserving the liquor. Melt the butter in a skillet and toss in the oysters. Stir-fry for no more than 40 seconds, depending on the size of the oysters. Do not overcook.

Toast the bread. Using a slotted spoon, remove the oysters from the skillet and pile them on the toast.

Pour the reserved oyster liquor into the pan, swirling it into the butter. Pour over the oysters and enjoy.

A lemon wedge adds a little extra *je ne sais quoi*, but it is the perfect complement to any oysters.

Serves 1

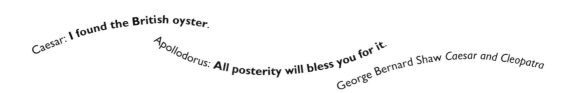

Caesar: **I found the British oyster**.

Apollodorus: **All posterity will bless you for it**.

George Bernard Shaw *Caesar and Cleopatra*

LOUISIANA OYSTERS

8 large oysters, about 3½–4½ ounces each

4 slices bacon, chopped

1 small onion, finely chopped

⅓ cup seeded and finely chopped red bell pepper

2 stalks celery, finely sliced

juice of 1 lemon

generous dash of Tabasco sauce, or to taste

salt and freshly ground black pepper

Preheat the oven to 325°F. Open the oysters, reserving the liquor. Remove the oysters and arrange them in a nonstick baking dish. Set aside.

Heat the bacon in a skillet until the fat runs, then raise the heat and fry until crispy. Add the onion, red bell pepper and celery, and cook until the vegetables are tender. Stir in the lemon juice, Tabasco and reserved oyster liquor, with salt and pepper to taste. Mix well.

Spread the mixture over the oysters and bake for 8–10 minutes or until the oysters are just cooked and begin to curl. Serve at once.

Serves 2

EASY OYSTER PIE

Make this pie in moments, using prepared puff pastry. The best oysters to use are *crassostreas*.

butter, for greasing

36 oysters

8 slices bacon

1–2 tablespoons oil

1 large onion, chopped

3 cups mushrooms, sliced

1 red bell pepper, deseeded and sliced or chopped

½ cup all-purpose flour

pinch of salt

pinch of cayenne pepper

¼ cup chopped fresh parsley

8 ounces puff pastry, thawed if frozen

Preheat the oven to 400°F. Grease a deep pie dish (2½ pint capacity) with the butter. Open the oysters, reserving the liquor. Remove the oysters and pat dry. Heat the bacon in a skillet until the fat runs, then raise the heat and fry until crispy. Remove from the pan and chop roughly. Set aside.

Add the oil to the bacon fat remaining in the pan. When hot, add the onion, mushrooms and bell pepper. Toss to coat in the fat, then cover the pan and simmer the vegetables for about 5 minutes. Stir in the flour, with salt and cayenne to taste, and add the reserved oyster liquor. After a few turns with a wooden spoon, fold in the oysters and bacon with the parsley.

Pile the ingredients into the pie dish. Roll out the pastry on a lightly floured surface and cover the pie with it. Cut a cross in the top so the steam can escape. Bake for 20–25 minutes or until puffy and golden.

Serves 4–6

OYSTERS ROCKEFELLER

I pound fresh spinach or frozen

12 oysters, opened, with juice reserved

½ cup finely chopped shallots

2 cloves garlic, crushed

2 tablespoons butter

I heaping tablespoon heavy cream

I tablespoon Pernod

pinch of hot red-pepper flakes or ½ teaspoon hot pepper sauce

½ cup grated Gruyère cheese

freshly ground black pepper

Wash the fresh spinach and place in a large saucepan with just the water which adheres to the leaves. Heat gently for 3–4 minutes until just wilted, drain well and squeeze out the liquid. Follow the package instructions for frozen spinach. Chop finely. Arrange the oysters on a flat, nonstick baking dish. Sauté the shallots and garlic in the butter, add the spinach, oyster juice and pepper. Add the cream and bring to a simmer. Purée the mixture in a blender. Return to a clean pan. Add the Pernod and pepper flakes (or sauce). Heat gently, to warm, stirring occasionally.

Spoon the mixture over each oyster and then sprinkle with the cheese. Place under a hot broiler until the cheese sizzles, about 2–3 minutes. Serve immediately with whatever you choose – tiny pasta shells go well.

Serves 2

"Why, then the world's mine oyster
Which I with sword will open."

Shakespeare *The Merry Wives of Windsor*

OYSTERS WITH SPINACH AND CAVA SAUCE

Cava – the Spanish answer to champagne – makes a superb sauce. If unavailable, use a good quality sparkling wine as a substitute.

1 pound fresh or frozen spinach

⅔ cup Cava (see note above)

2 shallots, finely chopped

⅔ cup heavy cream

24 Pacific *gigas* or 12 *virginica* oysters

salt and freshly ground black pepper

finely chopped parsley or chives (or both), to garnish

If using fresh spinach, rinse it thoroughly several times and place it in a saucepan with just the water that adheres to the leaves. Cover the pan and cook the spinach until just tender, then drain thoroughly and chop finely. Cook frozen spinach according to the instructions on the package; drain well.

Keep the spinach hot.

Heat the Cava in a deep skillet until simmering. Add the shallots and simmer for 3 minutes, then stir in the cream and reduce the liquid by half. Add salt and pepper to taste.

Open the oysters carefully, adding the liquor to the sauce. Set the oysters aside and scrub the bottom shells. Bring a saucepan of water to the boil, add the bottom shells and boil for 10 minutes. Drain the shells and arrange on 4 ovenproof dishes.

Divide the spinach equally between the shells, top with the oysters and cover with the sauce. Place under a hot broiler for 1 minute until the sauce bubbles. Garnish with parsley or chives and serve immediately with any remaining Cava sauce.

Serves 4

OYSTERS ROLAND JÖHRI – THE PASTA

This is an unusual pasta and is truly delicious; it is the first half of the recipe which is completed on page 38.

1¼ cups all-purpose flour

⅓ cup ricotta or fromage frais

1 egg, beaten

2 tablespoons melted butter

To make the pasta, place the flour in a bowl, make a well in the center and add the ricotta or fromage

frais, with the egg and melted butter. Gradually incorporate the flour and mix to a dough, then

cover and set aside in the refrigerator for 30 minutes.

Bring a large saucepan of lightly salted water to the boil. Shave the pasta dough in thin strips directly into

the boiling water. Cook for 2 minutes only, then drain thoroughly and keep hot.

Shucked oyster meat is sold in 2-quart containers in Louisiana, because they have such an abundant supply of oysters all year round. Packed in their own juice and well iced, these oysters will keep under refrigeration for at least 10 days – ideal for the cook who finds it difficult to open oysters, and a big bonus when unexpected guests arrive.

INDEX

American oysters, 10–15
Apalachicola oysters, 10, 46
angels on horseback, 26
aphrodisiacs, 16
au naturel oysters, 25

bacon: angels on
   horseback, 26
   easy oyster pie, 58
   Louisiana oysters, 56
baked oysters Australian
   style, 45
barley salad with oysters, 40
beef: beef and oyster pâté, 44
   carpetbag steak for the
   barbecue, 50
Belon oysters, 12, 30, 40, 54
Bon Secour oysters, 15
Breton Sound oysters, 11
Burlington Arcade,
   London, 54
buying oysters, 9

canapés, oyster and
   caviar, 28
carpetbag steak for the
   barbecue, 50
Carroll, Lewis, 26
Cava: oysters with spinach
   and Cava sauce, 62
Cavendish, Lord, 54
caviar and oyster canapés, 28
champagne, 23
cheese: baked oysters
   Australian style, 45
   forestière oysters, 46
Chesapeake Bay oysters, 10, 46

chilies: chili grilled oysters
   Mexico way, 42
chili sauce, 25
chips, oyster, 33
chowder, oyster, 30
Cole, Nat King, 49
crassostrea, 7, 9

drinks, 23

easy oyster pie, 58

forestière oysters, 46
freezing oysters, 25
fromage frais: pasta for
   oysters Roland Jöhri, 63

Guinness and oyster soup, 32

history, 17

jiffy oyster feast, 52

Kumamoto oysters, 13, 46

Louisiana oysters, 14, 56, 63

Mad River oysters, 10
mignonette sauce, 25
mushrooms: easy oyster
   pie, 58
   forestière oysters, 46

nutrition, 16–17

Olympia oysters, 7, 13, 28, 38
opening oysters, 9
ostrea edulis, 7, 9

pasta: for oysters Roland

Jöhri, 38; 63
pâté, oyster and beef, 44
pies: easy oyster pie, 58
   oyster pies in vine leaves, 48
poacher's breakfast, 26
Portuguese oysters, 7, 11, 42
pumpkin and oyster
   soufflés, 36

rice: jiffy oyster feast, 52
ricotta: pasta for oysters
   Roland Jöhri, 63
Rockefeller oysters, 60
Roland Jöhri oysters, 38

saffron: jiffy oyster feast, 52
salad, barley, with oysters, 40
salmon, marinated oysters
   and, 34
sauces, 25
serving oysters, 20
Shakespeare, William, 60
Shaw, George Bernard, 56
shrimp: jiffy oyster feast, 52
shucked oyster meat, 63
soufflés, oyster and
   pumpkin, 36
soups: oyster and
   Guinness, 32
   oyster chowder, 30
species, 7
spinach: oysters Rockefeller, 60
   oysters with spinach and Cava
   sauce, 62

Texas Gulf oysters, 15
toast, oysters on, 54
Tomales Bay oysters, 11
Totten oysters, 12

vine leaves, oyster pies in, 48

Wellfleet oysters, 14
Westcott Bay oysters, 11
wine, 23
   oysters with spinach and Cava
   sauce, 62

**Publishers
acknowledgements**
The publishers would like to
thank the following oyster
farms, fishmongers, people
and organisations for their
invaluable help :
Neil Duncan, Seacroft Oysters,
David Hugh-Jones, Atlantic
Shellfish, B & B Fisheries,
Loch Fyne Oysters Ltd.,
Duncan Geddes, Orkney
Seafayre Oysters, Giselle
Stroud, Seasalter Shellfish,
Islay Oysters, Carew Oysters,
Ross Lee, Bannow Bay
Fisheries, Nancy Griffen,
Chris Nelson, Bon Secour
Fisheries, Bob Wallace,
Billingsgate Fish Company,
Taylor United Inc.